# DIVERSITY, EQUITY, and INCLUSION CURRICULUM

By Mary Birdsell and Jo Meserve Mach
Photography by Mary Birdsell

### FINDING MY WAY
**The Finding My Way six-book series introduces kindergarten through 3rd grade children to both peers and adults with disabilities living inclusive lives.**

### DEI CURRICULUM
**With the social acclaim that *Everyone Matters*, it is important for students to learn about diversity, equity, and inclusion (DEI). As a literature-based study, this curriculum promotes DEI skill development by fostering student exposure to individuals living with disabilities and expanding their capacity to build relationships with all their peers.**

© 2021 Mary Birdsell, Jo Meserve Mach

These activities may be reproduced solely for classroom use and may not be used or posted online.

Finding My Way DEI Curriculum

Finding My Way Books
3512 SW Huntoon St.
Topeka, Kansas 66604
www.findingmywaybooks.com

(785) 273-6239

ISBN: 978-1-94754-136-8

Printed in the United States

10 9 8 7 6 5 4 3 2 1

For more information or to contact the author, please go to www.findingmywaybooks.com.

# DEI CURRICULUM                                    FINDING MY WAY SERIES

The **Finding My Way** book series presents diverse nonfiction stories that give voice to children with disabilities and promote their equity within our communities. Inclusive stories offer students the opportunity to meet children and adults with disabilities.

We arranged the six Finding My Way books into pairs for this DEI curriculum. Lessons link two books to explore a competency. Students will gain context for each competency by reading the stories, learning background information, answering discussion questions and completing activities.

## Diversity, Equity, and Inclusion

Competencies are the skill, knowledge, abilities, and behaviors that describe the standard to which a competent person is expected to perform...seven primary competencies associated with diversity equity, and inclusion:

- *Understanding Implicit Bias*
- *Microaggression Development and Understanding*
- *Cultural Competency*
- *Promotion of Civility*
- *Social Justice Development*
- *Organizational Learning*
- *Youth Development*

dei.extension.org

Begin and end curriculum with the **student survey** (page 34). Collecting this data offers you an opportunity to explore how the curriculum affected students' feelings about individuals with disabilities.

ABOUT THE CO-AUTHORS AND PHOTOGRAPHER

**Mary Birdsell** has authored nine children's books and is a former Speech and Theater teacher with an enthusiasm for all styles of learners. Mary believes everyone learns, creates, and has a story to tell. As a photographer, she strives to create images that reflect the strengths of each child. Mary's background in education, theater, and photography intersects as she visually creates each book. She uses colors and shapes to tell a story. For her, each book is like its own theater production.

**Jo Meserve Mach** is co-author of the Finding My Way Book Set. After working 36 years as an Occupational Therapist, she is very passionate about sharing the stories of children with special needs. Jo embraces the joy that individuals with disabilities bring to our communities through their unique gifts.

## Table of Contents

*I Don't Know If I Want a Puppy* and *Marco and I Want to Play Ball* ............................................................. 1
    Are You Being Civil? ............................................................................................................................. 3
    Being Ethan's Inclusive Friend ............................................................................................................. 4

*Kaitlyn Wants to See Ducks* and *I Don't Know If I Want a Puppy* ............................................................. 5
    My Feelings about Animals .................................................................................................................. 7
    Being Kaitlyn's Inclusive Friend ........................................................................................................... 8

*Marco and I Want to Play Ball* and *Waylen Wants to Jam* ........................................................................ 9
    Everyone Matters ................................................................................................................................ 11
    Being Isiah's Inclusive Friend ............................................................................................................. 12

*I Want to Be Like Poppin' Joe* and *OE Wants It to Be Friday* ................................................................. 13
    Having a Role Model .......................................................................................................................... 15
    Being Dylan's Inclusive Friend ........................................................................................................... 16

*Waylen Wants to Jam* and *I Want to Be Like Poppin' Joe* ..................................................................... 17
    Belonging ............................................................................................................................................ 19
    Being Waylen's Inclusive Friend ........................................................................................................ 20

*OE Wants It to Be Friday* and *Kaitlyn Wants to See Ducks* ................................................................... 21
    Secret Handshake .............................................................................................................................. 23
    Being OE's Inclusive Friend ............................................................................................................... 24

Isiah's Word Find ........................................................................................................................................ 25

Ethan's Word Find ...................................................................................................................................... 26

Waylen's Word Find ................................................................................................................................... 27

OE's Word Find .......................................................................................................................................... 28

Dylan's Word Find ...................................................................................................................................... 29

Kaitlyn's Word Find .................................................................................................................................... 30

**Finding My Way DEI Activities Key** ...................................................................................................... 31

**Student Survey** ..................................................................................................................................... 34

**Data Collection** ..................................................................................................................................... 35

**Inclusive Friend Award** ........................................................................................................................ 36

# DEI CURRICULM

## I DON'T KNOW IF I WANT A PUPPY
## MARCO AND I WANT TO PLAY BALL

*Genre*: Nonfiction
*GRL*: E
*Interest level*: Pre-K-3
*Lexile*: 240

*Genre*: Nonfiction
*GRL*: G
*Interest level*: Pre-K-3
*Lexile*: 350

*DEI competency*:
promotion of civility

*Disabilities represented*: congenital heart defect, speech/language delay, Spina bifida

*Themes*:
diversity, equity, inclusion, family

The **Finding My Way** book series presents diverse nonfiction stories that give voice to children with disabilities and promote their equity within our communities. Inclusive stories offer students the opportunity to meet children and adults with disabilities.

## Introduction
Ethan and Isiah both share stories about their families. Ethan tells about his immediate family with parents and older twin brothers. His brothers want a puppy.

Isiah tells about his extended family with his grandpa and cousin. He and his cousin Marco love to play ball with Grandpa.

## Diversity
Ethan and Isiah both have disabilities. Ethan has speech/language delays because of the extended medical needs and hospitalizations from his congenital heart defect. Isiah needed extra years to learn to walk and now wears leg braces because of his Spina bifida.

Isiah is biracial Black/White and Marco is biracial Hispanic/White.

*Diversity is a fact. Equity is a choice. Inclusion is an action. Belonging is an outcome.* David Robertson

## Equity
Ethan's family gave him an equal opportunity to take care of Emma, their new puppy. Because he takes the opportunity, he discovers he can handle the responsibilities.

Isiah's grandpa sets up a slide so he can slide in from the outfield and be more successful in his participation. Some boys might feel it isn't fair they can't run and so they won't play ball. Isiah plays to the best of his ability and has fun.

## Inclusion
Their families support both Ethan and Isiah in participating as fully as possible in-home activities. They want them to be included.

DEI competency: promotion of civility

# DEI CURRICULM

## I DON'T KNOW IF I WANT A PUPPY
## MARCO AND I WANT TO PLAY BALL

### Discussion Questions

1. What do you remember about reading *I Don't Know If I Want a Puppy*?
2. What do you remember about reading *Marco and I Want to Play Ball*?
3. What do Ethan and Isiah have in common?
4. What do you like to do with your immediate family and your extended family?
5. What are the similarities and differences between spending time with your immediate family and your extended family?
6. Do you tease members of your family?
7. How can teasing be civil?

### What Is Civility?

*Civility* comes from the Latin word *civilis*, meaning "relating to public life, befitting a citizen," in other words, being friendly and nice to everyone. **When you show civility, you use kindness and good manners**. You are respectful, even if you do not like that person very much. *Civility* can also mean formal politeness, like your behavior at a fancy dinner.
Vocabulary.com

## Activities

### Are You Being Civil?

Remember how Isiah and Marco tease each other when they play ball together? If you don't know the person teasing you, teasing can hurt. Isiah and Marco use their words to push each other to play the best they can. They also encourage and cheer for each other. Being civil means you are kind to each other.

This activity encourages students to think about how words can hurt. They evaluate sentences to identify if they are civil or not. Then, they write a civil sentence.

### Being Ethan's Inclusive Friend

This activity encourages inclusive thinking. Students identify two things they have in common with Ethan and two ways they could play together.

### Isiah's Word Find offers some extra fun on page 25.

DEI competency: promotion of civility

I Don't Know If I Want a Puppy and Marco and I Want to Play Ball

## *Are You Being Civil?*

Name_____     Date_____

Words can hurt. Cross out the sentences that are not civil.

You're stupid and can't hit the ball.

Good job.

I don't like how you hit the ball.

You're slow and never catch the ball.

You can do it.

I like playing ball with you.

No one will ever want you on their team.

You're nice.

You're a loser.

You can't play with us.

I'd like to be your friend.

You're fun to play with.

I don't like you.

You made a great catch.

Write a sentence that is civil.

_____

DEI competency: promotion of civility

I Don't Know If I Want a Puppy

## *Being Ethan's Inclusive Friend*

Name_____        Date_____

### Two ways I am just like Ethan:

1. _____

   _____

2. _____

   _____

### Two ways I would have fun with Ethan:

1. _____

   _____

2. _____

   _____

DEI competency: promotion of civility

# DEI CURRICULUM

## KAITLYN WANTS TO SEE DUCKS
## I DON'T KNOW IF I WANT A PUPPY

*Genre*: Nonfiction
*GRL*: F
*Interest level*: Pre-K-3
*Lexile*: 280

*Genre*: Nonfiction
*GRL*: E
*Interest level*: Pre-K-3
*Lexile*: 240

*DEI competency*: understanding implicit bias

*Disabilities represented*: Down syndrome, congenital heart defect, speech/language delay

*Themes*: diversity, equity, inclusion, communication

The **Finding My Way** book series presents diverse nonfiction stories that give voice to children with disabilities and promote their equity within our communities. Inclusive stories offer students the opportunity to meet children and adults with disabilities.

### Introduction
Kaitlyn and Ethan both like animals. Kaitlyn loves to see ducks at the zoo. Ethan learns he likes to take care of their new puppy.

### Diversity
Kaitlyn and Ethan both have siblings who are twins. Kaitlyn has younger twin sisters and Ethan has older twin brothers. Kaitlyn and Ethan both have disabilities. Kaitlyn has Down syndrome and Ethan was born with congenital heart disease.

*Diversity is a fact. Equity is a choice. Inclusion is an action. Belonging is an outcome.* David Robertson

### Equity
Kaitlyn and Ethan both are strong self-advocates. They have an awareness of what they want to do, and they do it. Ethan doesn't let his older brothers determine what he is going to do. Kaitlyn doesn't let her younger sisters determine what she is going to do. They both have parents who support their individuality and right to make choices.

### Inclusion
Kaitlyn's family doesn't tell her she has to stay home from going to the zoo because she only wants to see the ducks. Instead, they work hard to include her and her interests as they spend a family day at the zoo. They point out the water she likes and help her find the ducks in the pond.

Ethan's family respects that he may not want a puppy. Yet, they support him as he changes his mind. They include him in the family's decision to get a puppy, and then Ethan joins his family in caring for Emma. His family encourages Ethan by providing positive feedback when he helps Emma.

DEI competency: understanding implicit bias

# DEI CURRICULUM

## KAITLYN WANTS TO SEE DUCKS
## I DON'T KNOW IF I WANT A PUPPY

### Discussion Questions

1. What do you remember about reading *Kaitlyn Wants to See Ducks*?
2. What do you remember about reading *I Don't Know If I Want a Puppy*?
3. What do Kaitlyn and Ethan have in common?
4. What do you do when you see someone who looks sad?
5. How can you include an older sibling or a younger sibling?
6. How do you feel about animals living in your house or at the zoo?

### WHAT IS IMPLICIT BIAS?

"...implicit bias refers to the attitudes or stereotypes that affect our understanding, actions, and decisions in an unconscious manner. These biases, which encompass both favorable and unfavorable assessments, are activated involuntarily and without an individual's awareness or intentional control." *Kirwan Institute at Ohio State University*

## Activities

### My Feelings About Animals

We don't realize that we all have a bias about many things. We often base our feelings on our experiences. Sometimes, other people's reactions teach us a bias.

This activity gives students the opportunity to realize their feelings about animals and, as a result, their bias. Encourage students to generalize this thinking to how they may automatically feel about people they don't know, such as someone in a wheelchair. There are no right or wrong answers to this activity. It is about each student's feelings.

### Being Kaitlyn's Inclusive Friend

This activity encourages inclusive thinking. Students identify two things they have in common with Kaitlyn and two ways they could play together.

### Ethan's Word Find offers some extra fun on page 26.

DEI competency: understanding implicit bias

Kaitlyn Wants to See Ducks and I Don't Know If I Want a Puppy

## My Feelings About Animals

Name_____     Date_____

Circle a word and draw a line to the animal you think it matches.

Pick one word for each animal.

creepy

noisy

friendly

mean

scary

sweet

nice

soft

Pick one animal and its word: _____

Why did you match them? _____

_____

DEI competency: understanding implicit bias

Kaitlyn Wants to See Ducks

## *Being Kaitlyn's Inclusive Friend*

Name_____    Date_____

**Two ways I am just like Kaitlyn:**

1._____

_____

2._____

_____

**Two ways I would have fun with Kaitlyn:**

1._____

_____

2._____

_____

DEI competency: understanding implicit bias

# DEI CURRICULM

## MARCO AND I WANT TO PLAY BALL
## WAYLEN WANTS TO JAM

*Genre*: Nonfiction
*GRL*: G
*Interest level*: Pre-K-3
*Lexile*: 350

*Genre*: Nonfiction
*GRL*: J
*Interest level*: Pre-K-3
*Lexile*: 390

*DEI competency*: social justice development

*Disabilities represented*: autism, Spina bifida

*Themes*: diversity, equity, inclusion, community

The **Finding My Way** book series presents diverse nonfiction stories that give voice to children with disabilities and promote their equity within our communities. Inclusive stories offer students the opportunity to meet children and adults with disabilities.

## Introduction
Isiah and Waylen are both active in programs in their communities. Isiah is playing ball in his grandpa's backyard in his book, but he also plays on a community Little League baseball team. Waylen is learning to play on a community drumline.

## Diversity
Isiah, Marco, and Waylen are all biracial. Isiah is Black/White. Marco is Hispanic/White. Waylen is Hispanic/Black. Both Isiah and Waylen have disabilities. Isiah has Spina bifida and Waylen has autism.

*Diversity is a fact. Equity is a choice. Inclusion is an action. Belonging is an outcome.* David Robertson

## Equity
Isiah has a coach who supports him in being part of the community baseball team. Waylen is the first child with autism to join the community drumline program. Both community activities are competitive and require strong advocacy by parents to have children with disabilities accepted into them. Isiah and Waylen have the right to participate as do all interested children.

## Inclusion
The further children with disabilities move from their immediate family circle, the more challenge there is with inclusion. Isiah's mother encourages him to be as independent as possible in activities at home. She advocates for him to follow his love of playing ball. With the support of extended family, Isiah has gained skills to play ball on a community league. Waylen's older brother and mother advocated for his inclusion in the community drumline program.

DEI competency: social justice development

# DEI CURRICULM

## MARCO AND I WANT TO PLAY BALL
## WAYLEN WANTS TO JAM

### Discussion Questions

1. What do you remember about reading *Marco and I Want to Play Ball*?
2. What do you remember about reading *Waylen Wants to Jam*?
3. What do Isiah and Waylen have in common?
4. Why does everyone matter?
5. Should Isiah and Waylen be included in activities? Why?

### WHAT IS SOCIAL JUSTICE?

The objective of creating a fair and equal society in which each individual matter, their rights are recognized and protected, and decisions are made in ways that are fair and honest. *Oxfordreference.com*

## Activities

### *Everyone Matters*

Both Isiah and Waylen have to work extra hard to succeed at their activities. Isiah works on keeping his balance. Waylen works on staying focused.

This activity encourages students to think beyond the general stereotype of what is best. Instead, students can think about looking for other people's strengths and abilities. Everyone has something to offer. Everyone matters.

### *Being Isiah's Inclusive Friend*

This activity encourages inclusive thinking. Students identify two things they have in common with Isiah and two ways they could play together.

*Waylen's Word Find* offers some extra fun on page 27.

DEI competency: social justice development

Marco and I Want to Play Ball and Waylen Wants to Jam

## *Everyone Matters*

Name_____     Date_____

Choose one of these words to fill in the blanks.

| practice | catcher | nicest | help |
|---|---|---|---|

If you are not the best drummer, you could try to be the _____ drummer.

If you are not the fastest runner, you could try to be the best_____.

If someone has a hard time remembering a song, you could _____ them.

If someone has a hard time hitting the ball, you could _____ with them.

DEI competency: social justice development

## Being Isiah's Inclusive Friend

Name_____     Date_____

### Two ways I am just like Isiah:

1._____

_____

2._____

_____

### Two ways I would have fun with Isiah:

1._____

_____

2._____

_____

DEI competency: social justice development

# DEI CURRICULUM

# I WANT TO BE LIKE POPPIN' JOE
# OE WANTS IT TO BE FRIDAY

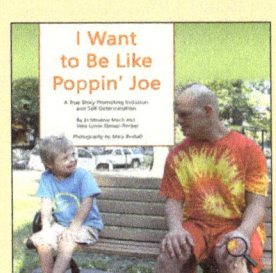

*Genre*: Nonfiction
*GRL*: H
*Interest level*: Pre-K-3
*Lexile*: 270

*Genre*: Nonfiction
*GRL*: K
*Interest level*: Pre-K-3
*Lexile*: 390

*DEI competency*: youth development

*Disabilities represented*: cerebral palsy (use of wheelchair and several communication devices), Down syndrome, autism

*Themes*: diversity, equity, inclusion, role models

The **Finding My Way** book series presents diverse nonfiction stories that give voice to children with disabilities and promote their equity within our communities. Inclusive stories offer students the opportunity to meet children and adults with disabilities.

## Introduction

Both Dylan and OE have adults in their lives who have disabilities and are very successful in their chosen professions. They both have wonderful role models to inspire them.

The US Senate recognized Joe Steffy as a successful businessperson with autism. Austin Hanson is a member of the US Paralympic Boccia Team.

## Diversity

Dylan, Joe, OE, and Austin all have disabilities. OE was born in Russia and adopted by an American family. Dylan and Joe have Down syndrome. Joe is autistic. OE and Austin have cerebral palsy.

*Diversity is a fact. Equity is a choice. Inclusion is an action. Belonging is an outcome.* David Robertson

## Equity

Joe and Austin both have jobs. Joe is a businessperson, and Austin is a competitive athlete. Many in society view people with disabilities as not employable and not capable of doing a job. Both Joe and Austin followed their interests and strengths to find a place they could be successful.

## Inclusion

When Joe was growing up, his small community saw him as different and as someone who needed to be kept separate from others. His parents advocated for him. Today, he represents his community with his popcorn business.

His peers saw Austin as someone with very limited physical abilities, someone they couldn't understand, and didn't want to know. His step-father became his coach and advocated for him to follow his mental abilities to figure out how to succeed as a professional boccia player.

DEI competency: youth development

# DEI CURRICULUM

## I WANT TO BE LIKE POPPIN' JOE
## OE WANTS IT TO BE FRIDAY

### Discussion Questions

1. What do you remember about reading *I Want to Be Like Poppin' Joe*?
2. What do you remember about reading *OE Wants It to Be Friday*?
3. What do Dylan and OE have in common?
4. What do Poppin' Joe and Austin have in common?
5. What does Poppin' Joe teach Dylan?
6. What does Austin teach OE?
7. What is a role model?

**WHAT IS YOUTH DEVELOPMENT?**
"...recognizes, utilizes, and enhances young people's strengths; and promotes positive outcomes for young people by providing opportunities, fostering positive relationships, and furnishing the support needed to build on their leadership strengths." *Interagency Working Group on Youth Programs*

## Activities

### Having a Role Model

Dylan and OE learn a lot from Poppin' Joe and Austin. What did Dylan and OE learn from their role models? Think about people in your life that you respect and learn from.

This activity asks students to identify skills taught by Poppin' Joe and Austin. It highlights what Dylan and OE learned. Also, students identify a role model in their lives and three things they have learned from them.

### Being Dylan's Inclusive Friend

This activity encourages inclusive thinking. Students identify two things they have in common with Dylan and two ways they could play together.

### *OE's Word Find* offers some extra fun on page 29.

DEI competency: youth development

I Want to Be Like Poppin' Joe and OE Wants It to Be Friday

## Having a Role Model

Name_____     Date_____

Draw a line from the pink ball to the items that Austin taught OE.

Draw a line from the popcorn to the items that Joe taught Dylan.

Austin taught OE how to:

Joe taught Dylan how to:

choose a ball

listen

work hard

direct a ramp

follow your interests

choose a ramp

Who is your role model? _____

What have you learned from that person? _____

_____

DEI competency: youth development

15

I Want to Be Like Poppin' Joe

## *Being Dylan's Inclusive Friend*

Name_____     Date_____

### Two ways I am just like Dylan:

1._____

_____

2._____

_____

### Two ways I would have fun with Dylan:

1._____

_____

2._____

_____

DEI competency: youth development

# DEI CURRICULUM

## WAYLEN WANTS TO JAM
## I WANT TO BE LIKE POPPIN' JOE

*Genre*: Nonfiction
*GRL*: J
*Interest level*: Pre-K-3
*Lexile*: 390

*Genre*: Nonfiction
*GRL*: H
*Interest level*: Pre-K-3
*Lexile*: 270

*DEI competency*: understanding implicit bias

*Disabilities represented*: autism, Down syndrome

*Themes*: diversity, equity, inclusion, belonging

The **Finding My Way** book series presents diverse nonfiction stories that give voice to children with disabilities and promote their equity within our communities. Inclusive stories offer students the opportunity to meet children and adults with disabilities.

## Introduction

Both Waylen and Joe were initially told they didn't belong. Before Waylen, the community drumline program did not allow children with autism to join. When Joe was young, the community swimming pool staff did not allow people with disabilities to get into the pool.

Waylen shares his story about learning to jam and what he learns when he is on the community drumline. Joe's story is told by a young boy named Dylan. Today, Joe is a very successful business person welcomed in communities all over the United States.

## Diversity

Waylen is biracial. He is Hispanic/Black and his drumline teacher, Sal, is a first-generation immigrant from Mexico. Waylen, Joe, and Dylan have disabilities. Waylen has autism. Joe and Dylan have Down syndrome. Joe also has autism.

*Diversity is a fact. Equity is a choice. Inclusion is an action. Belonging is an outcome.* David Robertson

## Equity

The communities where Waylen and Joe live accepted them into activities where they feel they belong. Waylen is an active participant in the community drumline. Joe's popcorn business sets up booths across the country at community fairs and other events.

## Inclusion

Communities include Waylen and Joe in activities they want to do because their parents advocated for them.

DEI competency: understanding implicit bias

# DEI CURRICULUM

## WAYLEN WANTS TO JAM
## I WANT TO BE LIKE POPPIN' JOE

### Discussion Questions

1. What do you remember about reading *I Want to Be Like Poppin' Joe*?
2. What do you remember about reading *Waylen Wants to Jam*?
3. What do Dylan and Waylen have in common?
4. What kinds of judgements do you make by looking at someone?
5. Are judgements always bad?
6. Do you have to like everyone else in order to belong?

### WHAT IS IMPLICIT BIAS?

"...implicit bias refers to the attitudes or stereotypes that affect our understanding, actions, and decisions in an unconscious manner. These biases, which encompass both favorable and unfavorable assessments, are activated involuntarily and without an individual's awareness or intentional control." *Kirwan Institute at Ohio State University*

## Activities

### *Belonging*

The first step to helping people feel they belong is to have others get to know them. This activity promotes that first step. It requires students to write the first name of every student in the class.

Also, it asks them to write something they know about them. For example, it might be their favorite food, favorite color, or their pet. It should be just one word.

If they don't know the other students, then the next step will be to facilitate a social exchange. Set students up in pairs to start conversations so they get to know each other.

### *Being Waylen's Inclusive Friend*

This activity encourages inclusive thinking. Students identify two things they have in common with Waylen and two ways they could play together.

*Dylan's Word Find* offers some extra fun on page 30.

DEI competency: understanding implicit bias

Waylen Wants to Jam and I Want to Be Like Poppin' Joe

## *Belonging*

Name_____    Date_____

This is a map of your classroom.

*Write the name of a student and something about that student in each square.*

|  |  |  |  |  |
|---|---|---|---|---|
|  |  |  |  |  |
|  |  |  |  |  |
|  |  |  |  |  |
|  |  |  |  |  |
|  |  |  |  |  |

DEI competency: understanding implicit bias

Waylen Wants to Jam

## Being Waylen's Inclusive Friend

Name_____     Date_____

### Two ways I am just like Waylen:

1._____

_____

2._____

_____

### Two ways I would have fun with Waylen:

1._____

_____

2._____

_____

DEI competency: understanding implicit bias

# DEI CURRICULUM

## OE WANTS IT TO BE FRIDAY
## KAITLYN WANTS TO SEE DUCKS

*Genre*: Nonfiction
*GRL*: K
*Interest level*: Pre-K-3
*Lexile*: 390

*Genre*: Nonfiction
*GRL*: F
*Interest level*: Pre-K-3
*Lexile*: 280

*DEI competency*: cultural competence

*Disabilities represented*: cerebral palsy (use of wheelchair and several communication devices), Down syndrome

*Themes*: diversity, equity, inclusion, communication

The **Finding My Way** book series presents diverse nonfiction stories that give voice to children with disabilities and promote their equity within our communities. Inclusive stories offer students the opportunity to meet children and adults with disabilities.

### Introduction
OE and Kaitlyn use nonverbal communication. They both have difficulty speaking. OE's difficulty in coordinating the muscles around her mouth and tongue makes it hard for her to talk.

Kaitlyn uses motions, facial expressions, and single word to communicate. OE has several communication devices that she shows in her story.

Austin is also nonverbal. Like OE, he is very smart and uses a device to talk. OE points a finger when she uses her device. Austin uses his nose to type his messages and then his device has a voice to share his message.

### Diversity
Kaitlyn, OE, and Austin all have disabilities. OE was born in Russia and adopted by an American family. Kaitlyn has Down syndrome. OE and Austin have cerebral palsy.

*Diversity is a fact. Equity is a choice. Inclusion is an action. Belonging is an outcome.* David Robertson

### Equity
Because OE cannot speak, using communication devices allows her to have equity in communication with others. Without the devices, she would have a hard time sharing her thoughts or completing her school assignments. Kaitlyn often uses her emotions to help her communicate with words or motions. They both can share their feelings and needs.

### Inclusion
Both OE's and Kaitlyn's families strongly advocate for them to take part as fully as possible in family, school, and community activities. OE needs special equipment, such as her wheelchair and communication devices, to help her participate.

DEI competency: culture competency

# DEI CURRICULUM

## OE WANTS IT TO BE FRIDAY
## KAITLYN WANTS TO SEE DUCKS

### Discussion Questions

1. What do you remember about reading *OE Wants It to Be Friday*?
2. What do you remember about reading *Kaitlyn Wants to See Ducks*?
3. What do OE and Kaitlyn have in common?
4. How does OE communicate her feelings?
5. How does Kaitlyn communicate her feelings?
6. How do you communicate your feelings?

**WHAT IS CULTURAL COMPETENCY?**
"...the ability to understand, appreciate and interact with people from cultures of belief systems different from one's own."
*apa.org*

## Activities

### Secret Handshake

The language you speak is part of your culture. Using sign language is part of some people's culture. Kaitlyn's twin sisters use sign language (p. 10 and p. 13), to share the names of animals. You can make up a language or secret way to communicate to create your own culture.

For this activity, students need to be in pairs to make up a secret handshake. Encourage students to use at least five distinct movements for their handshake.

### Being OE's Inclusive Friend

This activity encourages inclusive thinking. Students identify two things they have in common with OE and two ways they could play together.

### Kaitlyn's Word Find offers some extra fun on page 30.

DEI competency: culture competency

OE Wants It to Be Friday and Kaitlyn Wants to See Ducks

## Secret Handshake

Name_____     Date _____

Partner's name _____

Think up a secret handshake.

Think of a secret word to say. _____

When will you use your secret handshake? _____

_____

Draw a picture of you and your partner doing your secret handshake.

DEI competency: cultural competency

OE Wants It to Be Friday

*Being OE's Inclusive Friend*

Name_____     Date_____

## Two ways I am just like OE:

1._____

_____

2._____

_____

## Two ways I would have fun with OE:

1._____

_____

2._____

_____

DEI competency: cultural competency

Marco and I Want to Play Ball

# Isiah's Word Find

Name_____   Date_____

| | | | | | | | | | | |
|---|---|---|---|---|---|---|---|---|---|---|
| F | B | G | I | F | M | A | R | C | O | G | R |
| S | A | I | S | W | I | N | G | E | P | R | B |
| L | L | C | A | T | C | H | O | S | X | A | P |
| H | L | K | S | G | C | O | U | S | I | N | N |
| S | L | A | M | I | S | I | A | H | D | D | X |
| S | N | O | R | E | B | A | T | L | N | P | K |
| I | F | A | U | B | A | R | N | U | S | A | A |
| B | A | M | I | S | S | E | S | F | S | T | O |

Circle the following words in the puzzle. Words are hidden →  ↑

BALL          ISIAH

BARN          MARCO

BAT           MISSES

CATCH         SLAM

COUSIN        SNORE

GRANDPA       SWING

DEI competency: promotion of civility

25

I Don't Know If I Want a Puppy

## Ethan's Word Find

Name_____    Date_____

```
E  K  V  M  E  S  S  E  S  M  J  T
T  I  Q  J  C  O  K  R  O  L  L  Q
H  S  W  A  S  C  A  R  E  D  X  P
A  S  A  P  U  P  P  Y  W  V  P  S
N  E  L  G  L  A  D  Y  M  L  Y  A
T  S  K  A  O  U  T  S  I  D  E  D
B  R  O  T  H  E  R  S  H  M  N  X
Z  G  N  E  M  M  A  X  Y  I  K  H
```

Circle the following words in the puzzle.  Words are hidden ⟶ ↑

BROTHERS        OUTSIDE

EMMA            PUPPY

ETHAN           ROLL

GLAD            SAD

KISSES          SCARED

MESSES          WALK

DEI competency: understanding implicit bias

Waylen Wants to Jam

# Waylen's Word Find

Name_____     Date_____

```
S  A  T  T  E  N  T  I  O  N  W  S
I  J  A  M  M  I  N  G  N  Q  A  T
L  V  D  R  U  M  L  I  N  E  Y  I
L  K  B  E  A  T  R  I  C  K  L  C
Y  N  A  A  R  V  Q  N  Q  L  E  K
C  O  N  C  E  R  T  U  V  K  N  S
L  S  A  L  I  S  T  E  N  R  P  J
K  P  O  S  E  E  I  C  X  A  Z  C
```

Circle the following words in the puzzle. Words are hidden → ↑

| | |
|---|---|
| ATTENTION | POSE |
| BEAT | SAL |
| CONCERT | SILLY |
| DRUMLINE | STICKS |
| JAMMING | TRICK |
| LISTEN | WAYLEN |

DEI competency: social justice development

OE Wants It to Be Friday

## OE's Word Find

Name_____          Date_____

```
C  E  P  R  A  C  T  I  C  E  I  B
F  Q  A  J  I  S  I  C  K  R  J  O
R  W  B  A  X  X  X  B  A  L  L  C
I  Z  U  C  D  A  N  C  E  N  I  C
D  D  T  K  A  U  S  T  I  N  O  I
A  I  Z  E  S  C  H  O  O  L  J  A
Y  R  T  S  P  E  L  L  I  N  G  V
G  Y  M  R  A  M  P  N  F  V  J  H
```

Circle the following words in the puzzle.  Words are hidden →  ↑

| | |
|---|---|
| AUSTIN | JACK |
| BALL | PRACTICE |
| BOCCIA | RAMP |
| DANCE | SCHOOL |
| FRIDAY | SICK |
| GYM | SPELLING |

DEI competency: youth development

I Want to Be Like Poppin' Joe

# Dylan's Word Find

Name_____     Date_____

```
S  E  L  L  T  T  D  Q  L  T  B  D
P  O  P  C  O  R  N  J  E  W  S  U
N  X  X  M  T  W  O  R  K  E  H  M
D  Y  L  A  N  Z  K  N  V  I  O  P
R  A  K  E  B  O  S  S  X  G  V  P
Y  Y  V  J  U  G  G  L  E  H  E  Z
J  J  O  E  M  B  S  Q  G  N  L  K
Z  R  A  L  L  B  L  O  A  D  U  P
```

Circle the following words in the puzzle. Words are hidden ⟶ ↑

BOSS            POPCORN

DUMP            RAKE

DYLAN           SELL

JOE             SHOVEL

JUGGLE          WEIGH

LOAD            WORK

DEI competency: understanding implicit bias

Kaitlyn Wants to See Ducks

# Kaitlyn's Word Find

Name_____  Date_____

```
F  V  K  R  O  A  R  D  T  B  Z  H
A  K  A  R  N  P  A  I  G  E  O  U
M  S  I  O  Y  L  Z  Y  N  E  O  N
I  I  T  A  L  E  X  I  S  D  V  G
L  L  L  M  W  H  I  S  P  E  R  R
Y  L  Y  G  S  S  W  I  M  O  A  Y
N  Y  N  D  I  R  T  Y  A  V  U  N
D  U  C  K  S  I  X  C  S  P  Y  W
```

Circle the following words in the puzzle. Words are hidden →  ↑

ALEXIS            PAIGE

DIRTY             ROAR

DUCKS             SILLY

FAMILY            SWIM

HUNGRY            WHISPER

KAITLYN           ZOO

DEI competency: cultural competency

## *Diversity, Equity, and Inclusion Activities Key*

**I Don't Know If I Want a Puppy** and **Marco and I Want to Play Ball**

*Are You Being Civil?*
Cross out:
You're stupid and can't hit the ball.
I don't like how you hit the ball.
You're slow and never catch the ball.
No one will ever want you on their team.
You're a loser.
You can't play with us.
I don't like you.


**Marco and I Want to Play Ball** and **Waylen Wants to Jam**

*Everyone Matters*
If you are not the best drummer, you could try to be the <u>nicest</u> drummer.

If you are not the fastest runner, you could try to be the best <u>catcher</u>.

If someone has a hard time remembering a song, you could <u>help</u> them.

If someone has a hard time hitting the ball, you could <u>practice</u> with them.


**I Want to Be Like Poppin' Joe** and **OE Wants It to Be Friday**

*Having a Role Model*
Austin taught OE to:
choose a ball
direct a ramp
chose a ramp

Joe taught Dylan to:
follow your interests
listen
work hard

Finding My Way DEI Curriculum

## Isiah's Word Find

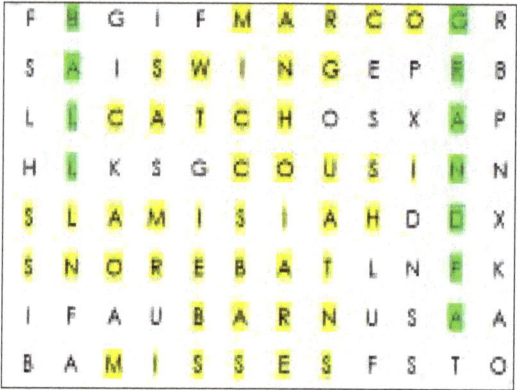

## Ethan's Word Find

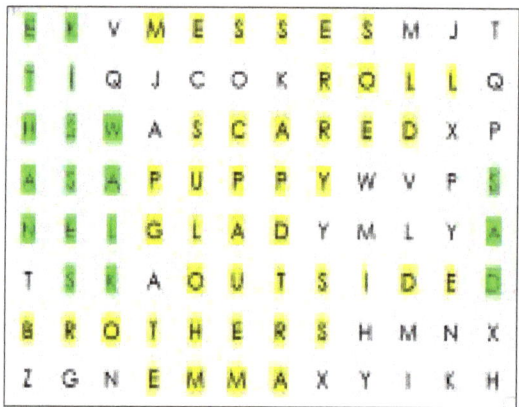

## Waylen's Word Find

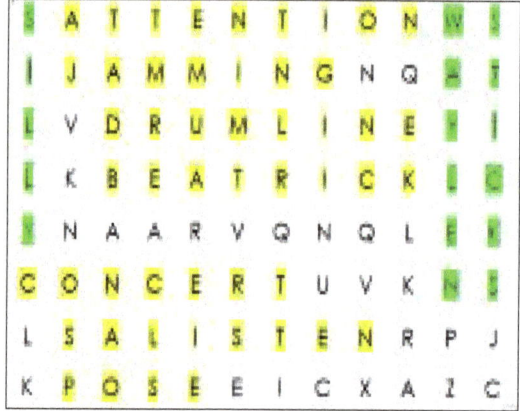

## OE's Word Find

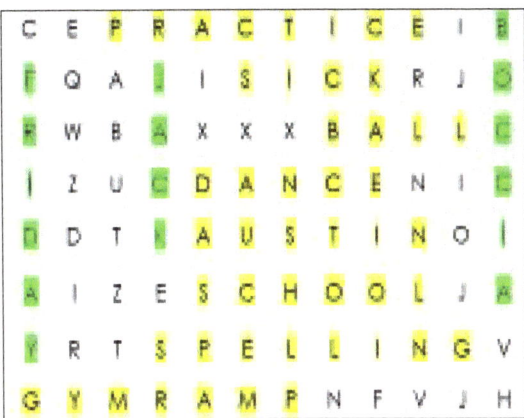

## Dylan's Word Find

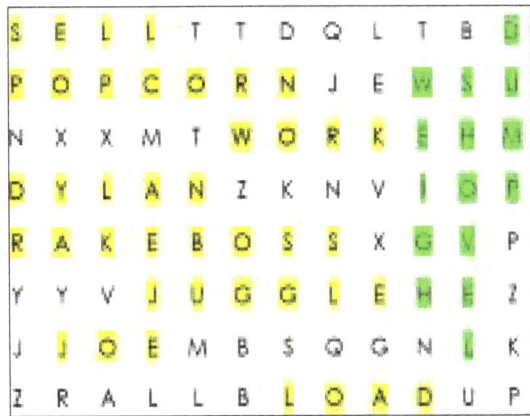

## Kaitlyn's Word Find

# Finding My Way DEI Student Survey

Name_____     Date_____

## Circle the emoji that best fits you.

|  | Don't know what to do! | Get nervous. Do nothing. | Smile | Talk |
|---|---|---|---|---|
| What do I do when I meet someone in a wheelchair? | 😳 | 😐 | 🙂 | 😃 |
| What do I do when I meet someone who looks different because of a disability? | 😳 | 😐 | 🙂 | 😃 |
| What do I do when I want to play with someone with a disability? | 😳 | 😐 | 🙂 | 😃 |
| What do I do when I want to talk to someone I know with a disability? | 😳 | 😐 | 🙂 | 😃 |
| How do I feel about being an inclusive friend? | 😳 | 😐 | 🙂 | 😃 |

# Data Collection for Finding My Way DEI curriculum

Organization: _____  Prepared by: _____

Number of participants: _____  Pre-survey date: _____  Post-survey date: _____

**Description**: Each survey contains the following questions with responses selected from an Emoji Likert type scale.

1. What do I do when I meet someone in a wheelchair?
2. What do I do when I meet someone who looks different because of a disability?
3. What do I do when I want to play with someone with a disability?
4. What do I do when I want to talk to someone I know with a disability?
5. How do I feel about being an inclusive friend?

**Scoring**: Each Emoji has an assigned value. Total the number of responses for each Emoji.

*Don't Know what to do! = 1*
*Get nervous. Do nothing = 2*
*Smile = 3*
*Talk = 4*

Multiply the number of participants X 5 questions to identify the total number of responses. _____
Divide the number of responses per Emoji by the total to get percentage scores.

Pre-survey:

- _____% of the responses were *'Don't know what to do!'*
- _____% of the responses were *'Get nervous. Do nothing.'*
- _____% of the responses were *'Smile'*
- _____% of the responses were *'Talk'*

Post-survey:

- _____% of the responses were *'Don't know what to do!'*
- _____% of the responses were *'Get nervous. Do nothing.'*
- _____% of the responses were *'Smile'*
- _____% of the responses were *'Talk'*

**Summary**: Compare the pre- and post-survey results to provide a general overview of change in participants' attitudes. For additional information you can score each question to identify more specifically where attitude changes occurred. Also, consider including anecdotal data and staff observations during the program.

# Finding My Way Certificate

**Diversity, Equity, and Inclusion**

## Inclusive Friend Award

For building an inclusive community one friend at a time!

**Awarded to**

_____

_____
*Signature and Date*